THE SNAKE THAT LIVED
IN THE SANTA CRUZ MOUNTAINS
&
OTHER OHLONE STORIES

TOLD & ILLUSTRATED
BY
LINDA YAMANE

OYATE
BERKELEY, CALIFORNIA

ISBN 0-9625175-6-9

Inquiries regarding requests to reprint all or part of *The Snake That Lived in the Santa Cruz Mountains & Other Ohlone Stories* should be addressed to the publisher.

Oyate is a Native organization working to see that our lives and histories are portrayed honestly and so that all people will know our stories belong to us.

Oyate
2702 Mathews Street
Berkeley, CA 94702
phone 510/848-6700
fax 510/848-4815
oyate@oyate.org
www.oyate.org

These stories are dedicated

to the many Ohlone people

of today.

May we flourish—

and be enriched

by these stories

from the past.

ACKNOWLEDGMENTS

First thanks and respect must be given to the elders who shared these stories so many years ago—Isabelle Meadows, Ascención Solórsano Cervantes, Barbara Sierras, and Manuel Onesimo.

Thanks also to Alex Ramirez, a valued friend, for his collaboration on the translation of "The Two Bears" story.

A big "thank you" to Native California Network for a grant that made it possible to spend the time necessary to complete this book—and especially for the deadline that forced me to do it in spite of a hectic life!

Sincere gratitude to the California Arts Council, LEF Foundation, and Threshold Foundation for making it possible for Oyate to publish these stories and give them back into our communities.

CONTENTS

ABOUT OHLONE LANGUAGES

You will notice that each story is identified, below the title, with the Ohlone language area from which the story originated. Because it is very difficult, and in many cases impossible, to reconstruct the many tribal (political) groups within the Ohlone area, most people today distinguish different Ohlone groups by language area.

These languages are all related, having some words in common, but also having differences, such as vocabulary and suffix variations. The language structure, however, is the same. Early European travelers recognized that the languages spoken by San Francisco bay area Indian people were essentially the same as that spoken in the Monterey area.

Modern language studies of Ohlone vocabularies collected in the mid- to late-19th century reveal that there were indeed differences—but the languages are clearly very similar. The Ohlone languages are part of a larger language category known as Penutian. The other California Penutian language groups are: Wintu, Nomlaki, Konkow, Maidu, Nisenan, Patwin, Lake Miwok, Coast Miwok, Plains Miwok, Sierra Miwok, Northern Valley Yokuts, Foothill Yokuts, and Southern Valley Yokuts.

Our neighbors to the south—the Esselen, Salinan, and Chumash—belong to the Hokan family of languages. The sound and structure of these languages are very different from Ohlone languages.

For those who may need clarification, the term "Ohlone" used in this book replaces the name "Costanoan" used more commonly in the past. I have chosen to use "Ohlone" because it is the name most often used by contemporary Ohlone people to identify ourselves, and is the term most likely to be recognized by the modern reader. The two terms are interchangeable, and refer to the group of people distinguished (at the time of European settlement) from their neighbors by language.

This map shows the approximate Ohlone language territories—Karkin, Chochenyo, Ramaytush, Tamien, Awaswas, Mutsun, Rumsien, and Chalon.

The boundaries have been deliberately diffused, as it is not possible to know with certainty where the languages transitioned.

The Ohlone's neighbors—the Coast Miwok, Patwin, Bay Miwok, Northern Valley Yokuts, Salinan, and Esselen—are included for context.

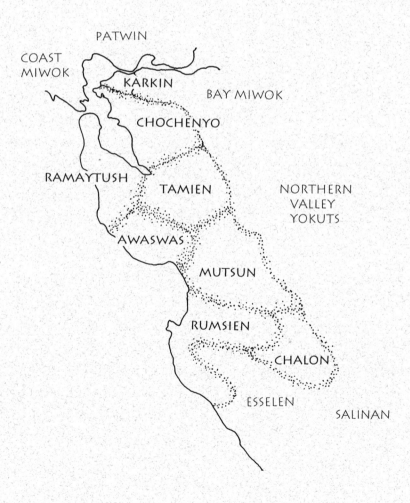

THE STORY BEFORE THE STORIES

That the following Ohlone stories are here for us today is a miracle, considering the repeated efforts, in the past, to stamp out Indian peoples and cultures in California. Beginning with the coming of the Spanish and their mission churches, Native peoples were looked down upon and our traditional ways were forbidden or discouraged. Later, when other Europeans, including Americans, migrated into California, the story was the same—Indian peoples were treated with disrespect and disregard, often very harshly, sometimes inhumanely.

Against great odds, these stories and others continued to be told among families and communities, and were still remembered by a handful of Ohlone elders in the late 1920s and the 1930s. At that time, John P. Harrington, an ethnographer and linguist working for the Smithsonian Institution's Bureau of American Ethnology, came to Monterey. He was looking for Indian people who still knew their language, history, and cultural traditions. He hoped to preserve their memories on paper before they passed from this earth, taking their memories with them.

In the Monterey area, Harrington located several Ohlone elders who were willing to share what they remembered. Sometimes they talked with Harrington for hours and hours in a single day. There are thousands of pages of handwritten notes, and from those pages came the stories in this book. Some of the stories were translated from Spanish. Some changes were made so the stories would flow, but the stories themselves are intact.

I would like to introduce you to these very special people. And I would like to thank them, for without them we would not have these stories today—stories that teach us and connect us to the world and people of the past.

Meet Isabelle Meadows. Isabelle was a speaker of the Rumsien Ohlone language, the native language that was spoken in the Monterey coastal area (including the lower Carmel Valley), at the time Mission San Carlos was established, and in later years. Born in Carmel Valley on July 7, 1846, the day the American flag was raised over Monterey's custom house, everyone had gone to town for the flag-raising excitement. "And when everyone came back, ya estaba yo aquí en este mundo [I was already here in this world]." At the ripe age of 85, Isabelle began working seriously with John P. Harrington, working long, 12-hour days on the language, folklore, history, and culture of the area. She even went back to Washington, D.C., spending roughly five years working with him there. It was in Washington that she died in her sleep at age 93. Isabelle shared "The Man Who Was Swallowed by a Whale" and "How Shelp Made the Acorn Soup"—two of the stories in this book. She told Harrington many other stories as well, some of which are included in *When the World Ended/How Hummingbird Got Fire/How People Were Made*, published by Oyate in 1995. Other stories still need to be translated, and I hope will fill future volumes.

Manuel Onesimo told "The Two Bears"—another of the stories in this book. The son of Juan Onesimo and Polonia Cruz, Manuel was born on a ranch just south of Carmel in 1861 and spent much of his life in Carmel Valley. He had not learned the native language of his ancestors, but knew other things, including several stories, that he shared with Harrington. Manuel Onesimo was the grandfather of my friend Alex Ramirez, who helped to translate this story several years ago. I remember when Alex and I sat side by  side in front of a microfilm reader, looking through page after page of Harrington's fieldnotes. As you can imagine, Alex was very touched to read the things that his grandfather and other relatives had said so many years in the past. He was even able to hear his grandfather's voice on recordings that Harrington made back in the early 1930s. We are certainly grateful today for the foresight of those of the past to preserve these priceless treasures.

In this photograph, taken in 1921, Manuel Onesimo (center) is shown holding the cornerstone for the restoration of the Mission San Carlos church in Carmel with his son Alejandro (right). Another son, Bertoldo, stands at his side (left).

Ascención Solórsano Cervantes, a speaker of the Mutsun Ohlone language of the San Juan Bautista and Gilroy area, was living in Monterey with her youngest daughter at the time Harrington began serious work with her in 1929. Ascención had spent years caring for the sick in her own home, but was by this time very ill herself and able to work with Harrington for only a few months before her death in early 1930. In that short time, however, Ascencion relayed vital information about Mutsun language and culture, and life at Mission San Juan Bautista. "How They Used to Make it Rain at San Juan" and "Trura—the Thunders" are two of the stories Ascención shared with Harrington. She also told the title story of this book, "The Snake That Lived in the Santa Cruz Mountains"—learned from her mother, Barbara Sierras. Barbara is pictured at right in a photo taken in 1902.

THE STORIES

THE SNAKE THAT LIVED IN THE SANTA CRUZ MOUNTAINS

AN AWASWAS OHLONE STORY

Long ago, there was a snake that lived in the Santa Cruz mountains. It came out of the sea, and would come up into the mountains, up into its favorite redwood tree. It had that tree smooth from climbing up and down so much—looking for people. It used to climb up there and look around, spying. And when it saw the Santa Cruz Indian people all gathered together harvesting seeds or acorns or something, it would give a loud whistle, and down it would come, dragging itself as quick as the devil to where they were.

That snake would surround them all in a loop, and squeeze them and eat them up! He didn't eat people a few at a time. No! He waited 'til he could get them all in a big bunch!

That snake was around there for so many years killing people and they couldn't seem to do anything to stop it. But, ah, the Indians were smart, as you will see, and they got to thinking how they might kill that snake.

The women got busy making baskets big enough to cover up a hole in the ground. The men started cutting down some trees and clearing the ground. And when the ground was cleared off and smooth, the men dug holes in the ground that they could get into to hide.

When the women had finished the baskets and the men had finished preparing the ground, some of the men went and each stood near a hole and placed a basket beside it. Others went to hide in the nearby woods. The men stood there, each beside a hole in the ground, so the snake would see them. Well, sure enough, that snake came and climbed up its favorite redwood tree. And when he saw all those people, he gave a whistle, and came down, lickety-split, to eat them up.

The men who were standing by the holes had their weapons, and those who were hiding in the woods had their weapons. When the snake came and surrounded them, the men who were by the holes jumped in and covered themselves over with the baskets.

The snake was so angry, he thrashed about and crushed all the baskets to pieces! Then the men who were in the woods came jumping out with their bows and their knives and they all attacked that snake. Those who were inside the holes were also stabbing it from below.

That snake was so angry. Oh, it was mean! Whenever it opened its mouth, some men threw handfuls of strong tobacco into the snake's mouth.

It was quite a fight, but they finally killed that snake. Then all the Indian people came around to look at it. They were afraid that snake might resuscitate— might come back to life. So, just to be sure, they cut that snake up into little pieces and ate it. Ever since then, we've never had to worry about that snake in the Santa Cruz mountains again!

THE MAN WHO WAS SWALLOWED BY A WHALE

A RUMSIEN OHLONE STORY

The Carmel Indian people used to tell the story of a man who was swallowed by a whale down near Los Angeles or Santa Barbara or somewhere.

By the time the whale got to the Monterey area, it was feeling sick and coughed the man out on a stretch of sandy beach at Point Lobos.

And do you know that when the man was first swallowed, he was dark? But when he came out of the whale, he was white!

It was ever since then that there began to be white people.

HOW THEY USED TO MAKE IT RAIN AT SAN JUAN

A MUTSUN OHLONE STORY

At San Juan Bautista, the medicine men used to have a little figure made of earth. They had it wrapped in a blanket, and when they had wrapped it up they tied it with cattail. Then they wrapped it in a cattail mat. After that, they wrapped it in a bigger mat, and then they wrapped it with more cattail.

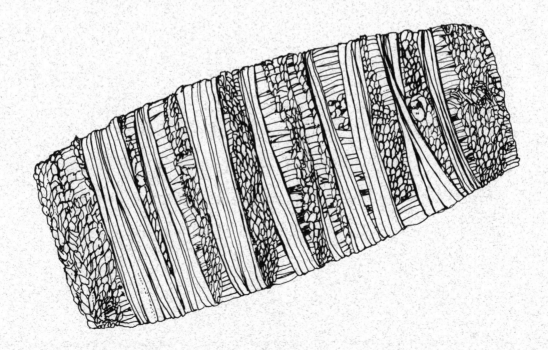

When they wanted it to rain, they would gather wood and go into the sweathouse and make a fire so the sweathouse would be good and hot.

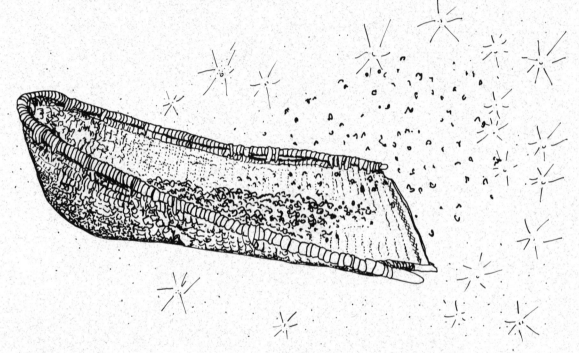

The old women had the seeds of many wild grasses which they used to gather, and they would carry those seeds into the sweathouse. The men would sing and dance and every time they finished a song, the women would throw a basket tray full of seeds into the fire. The fire would blaze and the seeds would pop.

Later, they would come out all hot and sweaty and would fling themselves into the creek, and then they would go back into the sweathouse. The captain would preach, and when he finished preaching, they would all start singing again.

Then they would unwrap the little figure until it only had the blanket on. Then they all went to the bank of the creek, taking along the little image.

The captain told the women to go home now, for it was about to rain.

They took the blanket off the little figure and the captain put it into the water. All by itself, the little image gave a few twists there in the water and floated away.

At the same moment, the men left for the sweathouse and only the captain remained.

That little figure was made of earth, but it didn't dissolve in the water—it always stayed the same. As soon as it made its journey, the little figure would come back and the captain would take it and put the blanket on it and take it back with him to the sweathouse.

There in the sweathouse, they would wrap it again just the way it had been, and they would sing and dance and burn more seeds.

At last, they burned a bear skin, and they kept singing and dancing—while outside it was raining.

HOW *SHELP* MADE THE ACORN SOUP

A RUMSIEN OHLONE STORY

Long, long ago, there was an old witch woman named *Shelp*. The people were having a big dance and *Shelp* made some acorn soup in her *SHEEwen*—her big pack basket.

"*Ay, 'AMmak*"* (Come, eat), she said to the people.

There were lots of people at the dance and just a little bit of acorn soup down in the pointed bottom of her *SHEEwen*. But no matter how much the people ate, that little bit of acorn soup never ran out.

When the people were full, there was still more. "Come, eat more," she told them.

"There isn't anymore," the people said.

"Oh yes there is," said *Shelp*.

You see, she always had more acorn soup in the bottom of her *SHEEwen*, because it was her witchcraft that was making it!

* pronounce: EYE, AW-mawk.

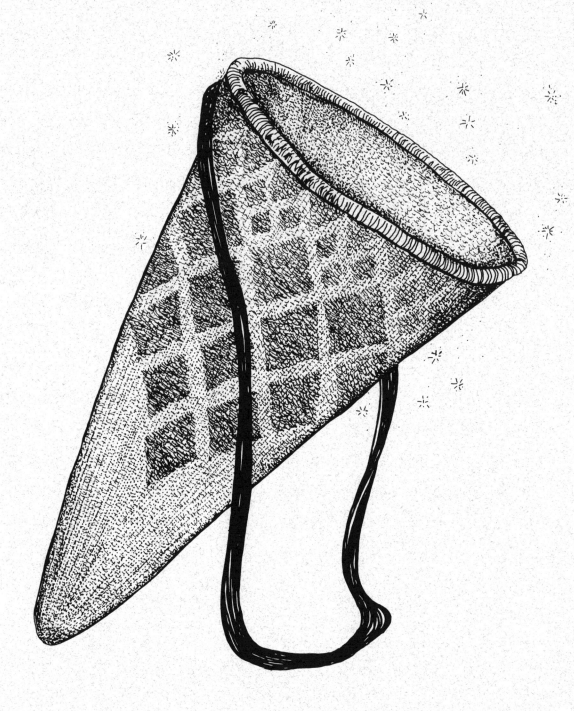

COMO LA *SHELP* HACIA
EL ATOL DE BELLOTA

UN CUENTO DE LA GENTE RUMSIEN OHLONE

Muy, muy antes había una vieja bruja llamada *Shelp*. Era una fiesta con mucha gente—bailando, cantando. Esa *Shelp* tenía su canasta de cargadora (con una punta abajo)—muy grande—que se llama *SHIwen*. Había un poquito de atol de bellota muy abajo en su *SHIwen*.

Toda la gente estaba comiendo de ese atol—comiendo, comiendo.

La *Shelp* les dijo, "*Ay, 'AMmak*" ("Vengan, coman.")

La gente le decía, "No hay más."

Y ella les dijo, "Si, hay."

Es que ese atol nunca se acabó, porque era la hechicera que estaba haciéndolo.

TRURA—THE THUNDERS

A MUTSUN OHLONE STORY

There was a widow woman, with two boys, and this mother was very old. She didn't have anything to give her sons to eat, and her boys couldn't do much yet because they were still young children.

And every time these poor boys went to the river where the men were fishing, the men would run them off. So when the other people would finish eating, these boys would go and find what they had thrown away. They would go up and down the river finding the castaway fish bones and they would pull the little nerve out from inside the backbone, like a thread. They would pull these out and put them in a clam shell—and they would go up and down the river doing this. And that was the food they would take to their mother to eat.

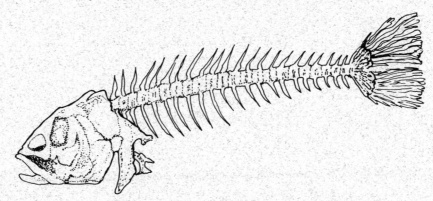

Then, don't you know, one day when they re-
turned from one of their trips they found that their
mother had died. There they were crying and crying—
and they buried her. They were so sad they just stayed
in the house. There was no one to give them anything to
eat and it seemed like they were going to die of hunger.

The younger one said to his brother: "Look, brother,
here we are just living so sadly. Wouldn't it be better if
we would go and make ourselves like animals that fly in
the wind, so that we could fly in the sky?"

"Well," the older brother said, "Just how do you
think you can do that?"

"I can do it," the younger brother told him. "But
look, whatever I do you have to promise to do also. When
I tell you to do something, be sure to do it."

It was like that every day. But the day arrived
when the younger brother began to bathe himself and
make himself ready. Then he said something like, "I'm
going to jump three times, and on the third jump I will
make thunder. Then I'll walk about in the sky." And so

he jumped, and sure enough on the third jump he flew and thundering, thundering, ascended up into the sky.

Then he told his brother, "Do the same thing!" So the brother started to jump, and jump, and when he jumped the third time, he also flew! But the older brother did not fly as fast as his little brother. He also went thundering up into the sky, but more softly, and joined his brother up there.

And so it is, that the younger brother thunders more violently, and the older very softly.

Remember those fishermen, who never wanted to give them anything to eat? They began to clap their hands and beg for forgiveness, for they had considered them worthless, that they were never going to be anything important. And now they had become "*Trura*"— the thunders.

When the Indian people heard the thunders, they used to say, "Listen, those are the brothers." For it always is that one thunders more loudly and the other more softly.

THE TWO BEARS

A RUMSIEN OHLONE STORY

Once—a long time ago—there were two bears and one said to the other, "I wonder how big the world is?"

The other answered, "Well, who knows? How are we going to find out?"

Those two bears were talking together and one said, "You walk that way, towards the south, and I'll go north. But we'll meet back here together again. Right near here we'll meet. You'll tell me what you saw, and I'll tell you what I saw along the way. Let's go. But each time you walk somewhere, give it a name. Give it a name so we'll know what it's called. I will, too. I'll do the same thing in all the places I go. Then we'll have to talk again."

So they went. I don't know how long they were gone. No one knows how many years it was before they met again at the Carmel River. But it was a long time

they were gone, and then they came back together.

"What did you see?" one asked.

"Oh," he said, "I saw many things. It was bad country, very bad, all of it. I passed by an ocean with black water. And I passed a huge river. It was very strong, and there were wild animals in the water."

They found that the world was very large, with lots of water, rocks, and ravines—everywhere—on both sides. But they gave every place a name.

And for many years after, those two bears were found talking together at the Carmel River, talking about all the places they had been.

ABOUT THE STORYTELLER

Linda Yamane traces her Ohlone ancestry to the Rumsien speakers of the lower Carmel Valley. She has devoted many years to researching the history, language, basketry, stories and songs of the Monterey area Ohlone people.

She lives in Seaside, California, and works as an author, illustrator, graphic designer and cultural demonstrator.